TEAM LEADER SKILLS

A Workbook on Leading Effective Team Meetings

Paul Preece

Team Leader Skills

A Workbook on Leading Effective Team Meetings

By Paul Preece

This workbook is published by:

Paul Preece

Lifelong Learning Solutions

19 Leyburn Close

Walsall

WS2 0NP

Email: p.preece@sky.com

About the Author

Paul Preece is a Management/Training Consultant with over thirty years' experience developing and implementing management and training strategies for prestigious companies for both SME's and multinationals.

Paul specialises in change management and has an outstanding record of designing and managing complex transformation programmes and turning around failing organisations.

He has extensive knowledge of organisational change that focuses on operational, teamworking, training, Lean Management, financial engineering, business strategy development, creating sales and marketing strategies and business process streamlining.

Progressing from apprentice through various management positions in different companies to General Manager/Director level, Paul has been part of, and led, teams at every level of the organisation.

Paul holds a Master of Philosophy Degree (M.Phil.) in research into business planning and strategy as well as other management, teaching and professional qualifications.

Table of Contents

INTRODUCTION

D oes this sound familiar:

'We have one scheduled team meeting a week where everything gets discussed - but the team performance just doesn't seem to get any better.'

We all know that meetings are a vitally important method of communication...and are a crucially important vehicle for decision-making in organisations - if they are run properly. Ineffective meetings not only impair organisational effectiveness by failing to meet objectives or make decisions but serve also to demoralise the people involved in them.

Time is money...and when you can't justify the time spent in team meetings when compared to the results of the meetings you have a major communication problem.

This workbook, with its probing questions, explains why meetings are far more than just a group of people discussing a broad range of subjects - and gives a blueprint for achieving superior results from your own team meetings.

Paul Preece is a change management specialist with experience across many different change management scenarios. What he did notice that, although different situations, the core problems of achieving significant results from team meetings were the same no matter what. That's when he set about writing this workbook – so that people could understand and grasp the fundamentals of making team meetings work for them.

The workbook presents the various stages of organising successful team meetings for your own situation through probing questions, tips for success, checklists and worksheets.

This workbook is primarily concerned with:

- The aspects essential to running effective meetings

- The vital role of the team leader

- The need to develop consensus in arriving at group decisions

HOW MEETINGS FIT INTO THE MANAGEMENT FUNCTION

A s shown in the diagram below, meetings are a microcosm of many factors making up the management function.

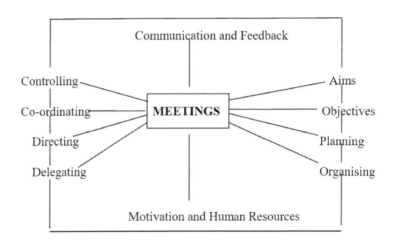

ACTION POINTS:

Meetings, both official and unofficial, are an important communication vehicle. Think of your current or previous experience and select one company that you have worked for. Answer the questions below and insert your answers in the spaces provided.

PERSONAL EXAMPLE

Company ....

Your Position ....

In what capacity did you attend meetings? ....

In your opinion, were the meetings (generally) led efficiently?
YES/NO

Were the results of the meetings (generally) productive?
YES/NO

How do you think that the meetings could be improved?

....

....

....

PERSONAL NOTES:

This blank space is for you to make notes on this section relative to the team/s in your own example. Use the notes in the text as guidance.

Additionally, consider what effect on the organisation as a whole did the meetings have? What additional resources were needed to improve the results of the meetings? How were other people's jobs affected because of the way that the meetings were organised?

WHY HOLD TEAM MEETINGS?

3.1 Introduction

A wide range of reasons can be identified for holding meetings. The majority are of direct operational significance but others are concerned with team building. The wider reasons include:

- Seeking information, ideas, suggestions and proposals

- Providing information regarding objectives, policies and plans

- Seeking and providing explanations and clarification

- Identifying problems and exploring difficulties

- Testing understanding

- Seeking confirmation and support

- Affecting attitudes by involvement

3.2 Meetings as a Team Building mechanism

It is vital that the role of effective meetings in Team Building be actively recognised.

The behaviours of a team in a meeting can give vital clues to its effectiveness in a broader organisational sense.

3.2.1 Indicators of Low Team Effectiveness

Some of the symptoms indicative of low team effectiveness that may be observed include:

- Hair splitting
- Ideas are presented but ignored
- Inability or reluctance to deal with the monopoliser, the arguer or the silent person
- Hidden agendas
- Sparring and one-upmanship
- Hard hitting humour
- Tough decisions are deferred
- Over reliance on the formal leader
- Playing games

3.2.2 Behavioural Indicators of High Team Effectiveness

- Contributions made within the group are additive
- Group moves forward as unit, are team spirited, and with high involvement
- Decisions mainly made by consensus
- Commitment to decisions is strong
- Group is clear about goals
- Group continually evaluates itself in an open manner
- Group generates new ways of thinking about things

- Members bring conflict into the open and deal with it

- Members deal openly with feelings

- Leadership tends to go (or move) to the person most qualified in the eyes of group members

ACTION POINTS:

Team meetings can be productive or destructive depending upon how they are handled. Think about your personal example from the previous section and answer the following questions.

Below are indicators of low team efficiency that come out at team meetings. Did these come out at the meetings in your example?

Company ....

Your Position ....

In what capacity did you attend meetings? ....

Hair splitting   YES/NO

Ideas are presented but ignored   YES/NO

Inability or reluctance to deal with the monopoliser, the arguer or the silent person   YES/NO

Hidden agendas   YES/NO

Sparring and one-upmanship   YES/NO

Hard hitting humour   YES/NO

Tough decisions are deferred   YES/NO

Over reliance on the formal leader   YES/NO

Playing games   YES/NO

What other low efficiency indicators came out at your meetings?

....

....

....

Do the same exercise for high team effectiveness indicators below.

Contributions made within the group are additive   YES/NO

Group moves forward as unit, are team spirited, and with high involvement   YES/NO

Decisions mainly made by consensus   YES/NO

Commitment to decisions is strong   YES/NO

Group is clear about goals   YES/NO

Group continually evaluates itself in an open manner YES/NO

Group generates new ways of thinking about things   YES/NO

Members bring conflict into the open and deal with it

Members deal openly with feelings   YES/NO

Leadership tends to go (or move) to the person most qualified in the eyes of group members   YES/NO

What other high team effectiveness indicators came out at your meetings?

....

....

....

PERSONAL NOTES:

This blank space is for you to make notes on this section relative to the team/s in your own example. Use the notes in the text as guidance.

Additionally, consider what effect on the organisation as a whole did the results of the team meetings have. Use the information in this section for guidance.

WHAT YOU NEED TO PREPARE FOR A MEETING

Team meetings are a vital way of organising day to day activities.

The team leader should have certain information available, such as:

- Next days and future projected production requirements

- Performance data

- Any potential production problem such as parts shortages, absentees, information, resources, customer data, etc.

Make sure the meeting is held where it is relatively private, but within team territory. Avoid interruptions.

Let everyone have their say, but control the creativity.

TALKING POINTS – THE AGENDA

It is a good idea right at the start of any team meeting to present any discussion points you may want to raise and ask if anyone has anything specific to discuss in the meeting.

A good way to begin is to look at what has been produced today and follow that by the needs (objectives) of the next day.

Then allow free discussion on any item the team wishes to discuss.

HOW YOU, AS TEAM LEADER, EFFICIENTLY CHAIRS THE MEETING

The following key points need to keep into consideration:

- The Team Leader's authority and influence not only comes from his / her position in the hierarchy but also from knowledge, from command of words with which to convey that knowledge and from an emotional power with which to impress and convince the meeting that it will be conducted efficiently.

- Persuasion can come as much from the Team Leaders sincerity as from the cogency of his / her arguments.

- State the purpose of the meeting, welcome everybody and outline the business to be completed.

- When time is crucial the timetable should be stated.

- When no time limits has been fixed the Team Leader should see that time is concentrated on the things which are really important.

- It is the Team Leaders duty to preserve order.

- Co-ordinate proceedings in a firm friendly but impartial manner

- Use tact and patience in dealing with irrelevancies but bring members back to point under discussion as quickly as possible.

- Encourage participation. Draw quiet members into active participation by direct questions, which should be easy to answer.

- Discussion should stem from a basis of fact

- Facts can be given in the Team Leaders introduction or the most knowledgeable member can be asked to begin the discussion with factual information.

- All discussion should be relevant to the question being discussed.

- Allow no discussion on matters outside the scope of the meeting.

- Check irrelevancies by asking the contributor how the interesting point he / she is developing relates to the topic under discussion.

- Discussion should be logical with reasons being requested. Attention can be drawn to faulty reasoning by asking how the conclusions follow from the facts.

- Use carefully phased interruptions to prevent the discussion being monopolised by a minority.

- Private arguments can be ended by asking the members concerned to let the meeting have their views.

- It is the Team Leaders responsibility to ensure that the discussions end within any time limit set.

- Contributions should be in a form that they are understood by all.

- The Team Leader should summarise at the end of the discussion each point.

- The Team Leader should not hesitate to intervene where necessary during discussion of a point, to summarise where agreement has been reached and where disagreement remains.

ACTION POINTS:

The emphasis on efficiently handling a team meeting is really reliant on the ability of the team leader/chair person. Looking at the points in this section, answer the questions below:

Look at the points in this section and list the characteristics and personality traits that you think that a Team Leader should have to chair a productive team meeting.

....

....

....

....

In the space below, give your own sample team meeting agenda for a meeting that you have attended. The meeting could have had a successful or unsuccessful outcome.

....

....

....

....

PERSONAL NOTES:

This blank space is for you to make notes on this section.. Use the notes in the text as guidance.

07

COPING WITH DIFFERENT TYPES OF TEAM MEMBERS

There are different types of team members:

- The quarrelsome type - likes to monopolise. Don't enter the argument. Let team pressure help control.

- The positive type - helps discussion and should be encouraged.

- The "always talking" type - again let the team "shut him / her up".

- The "shy" type - try to draw in this person - easy questions to gain their   confidence to take part.

- The uncooperative type - bring in this person by getting them to   contribute on their specialisms.

ALWAYS LISTEN - NEVER PUT DOWN - OR CRITICISE

- OR GIVE THE IMPRESSION YOU KNOW IT ALL

ACTION POINTS:

The above four categories are very definitive. In practice, the individual team member has a combination of traits. Handling this type of individual can be quite tricky. Draw on your past experience to answer the questions below.

In your past experience, have you come across these types of team members?   YES/NO

Did the Team Leader, or you, 'manage' these team members?

                                                        YES/NO

If the answer is **YES**, how did you do that?

....

....

....

....

If the answer is **NO**, using the text above, how could you have handled it?

....

....

....

....

PERSONAL NOTES:

This blank space is for you to make notes on this section.. Use the notes in the text as guidance.

Think about what you could have done differently concerning interacting with the different types of team members.

08

YOU NEED TO UNDERSTAND ATTENDEES BEHAVIOUR PATTERNS

These include:

- Active Listening   Display positive non-verbal response to the meeting and other participants

- Definition   Explain understanding of ideas and issues

- Re-definition   Explain one person's understanding of someone's explanation to confirm a common perception of the issues

- Listening and Linking   When a persons' turn to talk comes round they take account of what the previous speaker said

- Burning Issues   Not interrupting when someone else is talking because an idea has suddenly appeared in the mind.

- Building   Adding to what someone else has to say constructively

- Bringing In   Ask someone else for their opinion.

- Cutting Out   Avoid cutting across someone whilst they are talking.

- Taking Over   Avoid talking at the same time as someone else.

- Private Conversations   Two having a private chat should be stopped immediately

- Summarise   Where the discussion has got to especially if different perceptions / interpretations have arisen.

ACTION POINTS:

The different types of team members display different behaviour patterns during the meeting – and this includes the Team Leader – but it's up to the Team Leader to control the meeting. Think about meetings that you have attended, in whatever capacity, and answer the questions below.

What behaviour patterns do you recognise from the list?

....

....

....

....

Are there any other behaviour patterns that you have

....

....

....

Thinking about the behaviour patterns listed, and your previous experience, could you have done anything differently to guide team members more productively. If so, describe below how?

....

....

....

....

PERSONAL NOTES:

This blank space is for you to make notes on this section.. Use the notes in the text as guidance.

09

DECISIONS BY CONSENSUS
GUARANTEES SUCCESS

9.1 Introduction

Decisions taken by consensus, whether just in meetings or in a wider management context, have a much greater chance of successful implementation than if division is papered over by a majority vote. It is vital that all members of the group understand what is meant by consensus and the extent to which it should be sought.

The following is a realistic working definition:

"Consensus is the process whereby a group or management team fully explore a given problem, and possible solutions, in such a way that all members contribute to the best of their ability in the discussion and feel fully committed to the group / team decision(s)".

The presence of consensus within a working group should evoke a strong personal feeling towards the decisions made and the people who have shaped them, even where the individual may not totally agree with either. This feeling can be expressed as follows:-

"I understand what most of you would like to do. I personally would not do that, but I feel that you understand what my alternative would be. I have had sufficient opportunity to sway you to my point of view but clearly have not been able to do so.

Therefore I will gladly go along with what most of you wish to do".

9.2 In Search of Consensus

The search for consensus involves both the group and individuals within it adopting roles, attitudes and behavioural patterns. A range of guidelines for obtaining consensus is given below:-

- Avoid taking up an entrenched position in defence of individual judgements.

- Approach the task on the basis of logical and rational evaluation of information and opinions.

- Avoid changing of minds only in order to reach an agreement or to avoid conflict.

- Individuals should support only solutions with which they are at least able to agree partially. Avoid "conflict reducing" techniques such as majority vote, averaging or trading in reaching a decision.

- View differences of opinion as helpful rather than as a hindrance in decision making.

- Allow, indeed encourage, all members to express their opinions.

- Personalise individual contribution to the group by using 'I' rather than general words such as "we, one, they, people".

- Adopting the first person will demonstrate ownership of ideas and beliefs, thus permitting others to define the owner as a unique person and encouraging others to do the same.

- All should listen actively to the contributions of others and practice "checking" whether what was said was fully understood.

- Avoid making instant assessments of statements; practice "clarifying" what was heard before pronouncing on it.

- Practice giving feedback to others on their behaviour and attitudes and encourage a two-way flow.

ACTION POINTS:

Getting all people to agree with a decision is no mean feat. But it really is the only sure fire way of getting things done – and the crux of a successful outcome of a team meeting. Consider the information in Sections 3 to 9 and answer the following questions.

What do you consider to be the main factor in gaining consensus?

....

....

....

....

Do you consider that the Team Leader is a major influencing factor in gaining consensus?   *YES/NO*

If the answer is YES then how can they best ensure that consensus is achieved?

....

....

....

....

What other factors do you consider to be key in reaching consensus?

....

....

....

....

PERSONAL NOTES:

This blank space is for you to make notes on this section. Use the notes in the text as guidance.

10

PRODUCTIVE OUTCOMES FROM YOUR EFFICIENTLY RUN MEETING

L ooking at a meeting the participants should see that:

- Objectives were clearly understood and accepted and members worked constructively towards those objectives.

- Members approached the problem systematically. A method of approach was quickly agreed and they adhered to it unless it was deliberately changed.

- The meeting used its resources to the full and showed itself capable of adapting to any new challenge.

- Members were frank, open, tolerant and confident of each others sincerity. Feelings were fully expressed.

- Decisions were well considered, based on facts and reasons and were reached by a consensus in which everybody was free to present their feelings and thoughts and have them listened to. Decisions were not compromises, forced, or steam-rollered.

- Points of disagreement were thrashed out logically until all members were satisfied. Tempers controlled and reason prevailed over emotions.

ACTION POINTS:

The whole point of you going through this workbook is to get to this point – where you can get productive outcomes from your team meetings. Using the information in the various sections of this workbook answer the following questions.

Do you think that any other productive outcomes should be added to the above list? **YES/NO**

If YES, what additional points are they?

....

....

....

....

From your own point of view, what do you need to focus on to make your meetings more productive?

....

....

....

....

PERSONAL NOTES:

This blank space is for you to make notes on this section.. Use the notes in the text as guidance.

Think about why your meetings were unsuccessful AND successful. What could you have done to improve the meeting outcomes?

Printed in Great Britain
by Amazon